The Saxon Shore

The Romans in Britain built a massive early-warning system of fortresses, lookouts and signal towers along the North Sea coast — which they called the Saxon Shore. 'Saxon' because it faced the Saxon menace, but also because communities of Germanic origin were already living there. These 'Roman British Saxons' were truly an uprooted people: fully Saxon no more, never Roman, and certainly not British in the native sense. When Rome fell in 410, these 'plantationer' communities were left naked to the British aftermath. It is with one such community that the play is concerned.

'What impresses with *The Saxon Shore* is the way every detail and dimension of the play has an immediate meaning yet is richly metaphorical . . . It is Rudkin's power to engage with public crisis as it affects the roots of individuality that makes this play such a monumental work of the imagination.'

Richard Allen Cave, *THES*

DAVID RUDKIN was born in 1936. After King Edward's School, Birmingham, the Royal Corps of Signals, and Saint Catherine's, Oxford, he taught Latin, Greek and Music at a County High School in Worcestershire until 1964. His first performed play was for Radio in 1960, *No Accounting for Taste, Afore Night Come* was staged by the Royal Shakespeare Company in 1962 and subsequently in Germany, Sweden and the USA. There followed several television plays, *The Stone Dance* (1963), *Children Playing* (1967), *House of Character* (1968), *Blodwen, Home from Rachel's Marriage* (1969), *Bypass* (1972), *Atrocity* (1973) and *Penda's Fen* (1974), a short stage play, *The Filth Hunt* (Almost Free Theatre, 1972), a comic opera libretto, *The Grace of Todd* (Aldeburgh Festival, 1969; composer, Gordon Crosse), and two more radio plays, *Gear Change* (1967) and *Cries from Casement as His Bones are Brought to Dublin* (1973), which was also staged by the RSC (1973). *Ashes* was his second full-length original play to be staged (Open Space Theatre, 1974, and subsequently world-wide), though his next, *The Sons of Light* (Tyneside Theatre Company, 1975; revised for the RSC in 1976) was first written in 1965. Recent work has included two translations of Euripides, *Hecuba* for radio (1975) and *Hippolytus* for the RSC (1978), two stage plays, *Hansel and Gretel* (RSC, 1980) and *The Triumph of Death* (Birmingham Repertory Theatre, 1981), and the television film *Artemis 81,* screened in 1981.

DAVID RUDKIN

The Saxon Shore

A METHUEN PAPERBACK

A METHUEN MODERN PLAY

First published in Great Britain as a paperback original
in 1986 by Methuen London Ltd, 11 New Fetter Lane,
London EC4P 4EE.

Copyright © 1986 by David Rudkin

British Library Cataloguing in Publication Data

Rudkin, David
  The Saxon Shore.— (Methuen modern
  plays series)
  I. Title
  822'.914   PR6068.U75

  ISBN 0-413-14100-4

CAUTION

All rights whatsoever in this play are strictly reserved and
application for performance etc, should be made before rehearsal
to Margaret Ramsay Ltd., 14a Goodwin's Court, St. Martin's
Lane, London WC2N 4LL. No performance may be given unless
a licence has been obtained.

This book is sold subject to the condition that it shall not, by
way of trade or otherwise, be lent, resold, hired out or otherwise
circulated without the publisher's prior consent in any form of
binding or cover other than that in which it is published and
without a similar condition including this condition being
imposed on the subsequent purchaser.

Set in IBM 10pt Journal by 🅵 Tek-Art, Croydon, Surrey
Printed in Great Britain

AN HISTORICAL NOTE

The Celts were not the first people in these islands. But they were certainly here in the Bronze Age. Later, in the Iron Age, a Belgic people came. These confined themselves mainly to the more easily tilled 'lowland zone' south-east of the Cotswold limestone ridge. Within this corner, they mixed with the Celts, and established powerful local kingdoms. It was with such Belgo-Celtic British kings as these that Julius Caesar dealt. Meanwhile, north and west of the Cotswold ridge, in the rougher and more difficult 'upland zone', the 'native' Celtic culture continued more or less unmixed.

The Roman conquest, of the 1st century AD, also confined itself within the natural Cotswold boundary. From Axmouth to Lincoln the Romans fortified the limestone ridge against the British natives north and west, and this frontier rampart survives as the Fosse Way road-route to this day. (To this day, also, the Cotswold upland plateau remains the principal economic frontier between the south-eastern 'home' counties and the rest.) The harsher land, north and west, Roman generals and surveyors came to know as 'Lesser Britain'.

For Rome sought to conquer this 'lesser' Britain too. Soon the legions were pushing north and west beyond the Fosse, and by the mid 70s AD had established a legionary city at Gloucester. Though here, in *Glevum,* they Latinized, as always, a native Celtic name, in effect they had divided the western Celtic territory in two, the *cwms* of Wales from the *combes* of Devon, with the Severn estuary and Bristol Channel in between. This severing was to be for ever. Northward, the emperor Hadrian established a further frontier, across the Tyne-Solway isthmus, and during the 120s he fortified this with a wall. A subsequent advance, toward the Forth-Clyde isthmus, could not be maintained; attempts to conquer 'Scotland' were soon abandoned: and throughout the rest of the Empire period Rome's writ in Britain was to end at this wall.

Within the Roman province of Britannia, mostly the Celtic British and the Romans mingled and fused. But we must never make the mistake of thinking of the 'Romans' as one single people. They were individuals from many different parts of the Roman Empire, drafted here and settling here. Toward the end of the Empire period, the 'Romans' who came here, even up on Hadrian's Wall, could be personnel from quite exotic places. Beyond that frontier, meanwhile, the Celts who dwelled in the even wilder landscapes to the north, or had migrated or been driven there, remained alienated from Rome; and when, toward the end of the 4th century, Roman power began to weaken, some of these Celtic peoples became restless again, and started southward, to threaten, attack, and breach the Wall. Along the best-preserved, central section of the Wall, hasty repairs that the Romans did can still be seen. Soon other Celts, from Ireland, were raiding the western coasts, of 'Cumbria' and Wales. And a third, new force appeared on the scene: 'Saxon' pirates from across the North Sea. In AD 367, attacks from Scotland, Ireland and the North Sea coincided. It was probably not a 'collusion of savages' as one late Roman writer seems to have called it; but new movements and forces were at work, and the Roman presence in Northern Britain never quite recovered. It is against this background, of 'trouble' in the northern province of 'Lesser Britain', that the play is set.

'Saxon' was the general Roman term for peoples of North German origin. Among these Germanic peoples there was a great migration under way. These 'Saxons' never invaded Britain in the systematic intentional sense that the Romans had. From 367 onward, they came in waves. But the evidence is, that it was the Romans who first brought them here.

Rome's immediate response to the crisis of 367 had been to fortify the North Sea coast. Under the remarkable, and ruthless, general Theodosius — he was also something of a Christian commissar — a great system of shore-fortresses and beacon-towers was established, from Portsmouth in the south to Flamborough in the north; and the remains of a somewhat later fortress-tower on the coast of Durham can be seen. This early-warning system appears in Roman official documents under the designation *Litus Saxonicum,* and we know of a special military command

whose sole responsibility was this 'Saxon Shore'. Why the
Romans called that shore 'Saxon' is still disputed. Because it
faced the Saxon menace? Or because 'Saxons' were already living
there? The Latin could mean either; but in effect both meanings
applied. That the shore 'faced' the Saxons is not in doubt; but we
also have archaeological evidence of Germanic communities
already living in Eastern Britain during this late Roman period.
That fits with what we know of Roman imperial practice. Entire
peoples could be transplanted from one part of the Empire to the
other, to help in the defence of threatened territories. We have
accounts of whole Germanic communities being deported in
chains. So, whatever the later 'Saxons' did in this island to
deserve the bad press the early Celtic literature gives them (and
'Saxon' remains to this day the basic Celtic word for an
'Englishman'), the likelihood almost certainly is that the very
first 'Saxons' to come here were brought by Rome and planted
here: uprooted from their own lands, brought in misery and
bondage to a neighbouring island to serve the Empire's cause;
then, when Empire's need of them was done, abandoned against
the aftermath.

I have taken my cue from this. My only (conscious) bending of
history has been to telescope slightly the geography of Northern
Britain, to bring one such plantationer 'Saxon' community
beneath the Roman Wall itself. I have also, for the purpose of
the play, assumed that Rome's 'last' emperor, Honorius, actually
did write a letter 'to the cities of Britain, telling them to look to
their own defence'. This story is deeply ingrained in tradition, but
our sole source for it is a half-sentence in a very poor Byzantine
historian who wrote at second-hand and often transcribed the
names of places wrongly. For all that, the incident is too good a
dramatic opportunity to miss.

But before any 'Saxons' came, before even the Romans or the
Belgic people came, the native Celtic Britons of this island spoke
their own language, and that language survived. The British Celts
referred to themselves as *Cumri,* which means 'our kind'. Their
Cumric language derived from the Indo-European proto-language,
emerging in the same 'generation' as Latin, Greek and Sanskrit.
At the time in which this play is set, Cumric had as much
complexity as its cousin Latin had, and in many elements of

grammar and vocabulary it was very similar. In fact, being an isolated language, and not subject to the worldwide usage and abusage Latin was, Cumric would at this time have been more archaic and conservative. When Rome left, so far from reasserting itself as the native language of Britain, Cumric found itself in retreat before two new threats: the Saxon advance, and the missionary spread of the 'new' Latin of the Christian Church. Cumric underwent a colossal upheaval. Within two centuries, all its word-form endings — of the *-us -a -um* variety — were shed, leaving only traces of themselves in the sounds that survived. (That is why, in certain combinations, many Celtic words 'mutate' their initial consonants to this day.) By about AD 650, this British Celtic language is already recognizable as the direct ancestor of the 'Welsh' of Wales, the 'Cornish' of 'Corn-Wales', and the 'Breton' of the 'Britanny' to which migrating Britons of Corn-wall brought it. But the British Celts of Roman times left no written literature. Only by applying the laws of language-evolution in reverse, working backwards from the earliest 'Welsh' texts and inscriptions that we have, and from the names of places and rivers, can we recover anything of what the British spoke. Some tentatively reconstructed 'Cumric' is heard in the play. (I am indebted here to the magnificent *Language and History in Early Britain* of Kenneth Jackson, and other works of scholarship referred to there.)

For dramatic reasons, the last four years of 'Roman Britain' have been compressed into a single winter.

DR

. . . Behold, I, even I, do bring a flood of waters upon the earth, to destroy all flesh . . . Everything that is in the earth shall die. But with thee will I establish my covenant; and thou shalt come into the ark, thou, and thy sons . . .

Genesis 6: 17, 18

The Saxon Shore was first presented at the Almeida Theatre, London, on 27th February 1986, with the following cast:

MOTHER ATHDARK	Pauline Delaney
CAMBYSES OLD FARMER LLYR	Robert Eddison*
WIDOW FLAX SULGWEN PRISCILLINA	Brenda Fricker
AGRICOLA LUGOVELIN	Jonathan Kent
ATHDARK	Gerard Murphy
AGNES CEIRIAD	Joely Richardson
LITORIUS ROMAN NCO	John Rogan

Directed by Pierre Audi
Designed by Hildegard Bechtler
Lighting by Jean Kalman
Original Music by Oliver Knussen

*These roles were taken over at short notice by Ian McDiarmid owing to the sudden illness of Robert Eddison.

Notes on the Casting:

In order of appearance:

CAMBYSES, *Leader of the Nine of Werewolves. He is presumably the* OLD FARMER *by day. The same actor also appears as the dead* LLYR, *King of Britain.*

The wolf LITORIUS *is the Roman-British Squire by day. As wolf, his speech is rural. The same actor plays also the* ROMAN NCO.

The wolf AGRICOLA *is the Saxon community's Pastor by day. The same actor plays also* LUGOVELIN, *Prince of Britain.*

The wolf AGNES *is the Pastor's wife by day. She is pregnant. The same actress plays also* CEIRIAD, *the British princess, later Queen.*

The fourth wolf is ATHDARK.

MOTHER ATHDARK, *his mother.*

The WIDOW FLAX *is later seen as a wolf by night. The same actress plays also* SULGWEN, *the British priestess and nurse to Ceiriad. She plays also* PRISCILLINA, *the Squire's wife.*

The play is set near a remote part of Hadrian's Wall, winter-spring, AD 410.

PART ONE

ACT ONE

Scene One

Darkness. Nightsound: peewit alarmcry, snap of a twig — phwwwy phwwwy, tik tik tik . . . Lord of the forest CAMBYSES *waits, about him werewolves soundlessly gathering.*

CAMBYSES (*old, rasping*). Are we all safe? Are we all returned?

ONE. Ay Master. (*Male, middle-aged:* LITORIUS.)

CAMBYSES. Work done?

A SECOND. Well done. (*Male, young:* AGRICOLA.)

A THIRD. God's work! (*Female, young:* AGNES.)

ALL OF THEM. Eh-men! Eh-men!

But a FOURTH WOLF *is silent.*

CAMBYSES. Have we left the British cause for tears?

AGRICOLA. Ay Lord! When grey light comes, they'll know their loss. 'My child! My baby! My daughter, my wife! My son! Haowwl! Haowwl! The wolves were here!'

AGNES. That we were.

OTHERS. Eh-men!

But FOURTH WOLF *silent.*

CAMBYSES. What have we done?

AGNES. I fell on a farmstead. Out beyond Turfmires. The farmer's little son came out to see what 'noise was. He saw my eyes. My yellow eyes. He sank to his knees. 'Good wolf! Please! No!' I understood his British language! I dragged he off among the thorns. I tore the flesh from his bones wi' teeth and claws. I feasted on he all. But 'shoulder and the stomach part.

CAMBYSES. Good sister. One Briton less, to sow his rebel seed.

AGRICOLA. Master? I tore a woman from her bed. Down Pigsty

Valley. Too large to drag far. I gashed her throat, kicked in her head. One woman less for Brit to breed by. Master, see. (*Maw, dripping blood.*)

CAMBYSES. Good, brother; good.

LITORIUS. Lord? Sir? A white ewe-lamb had been the sweetest I had ate till now, and lapped its blood. But nothing so sweet as tonight. A British baby from its cradle. Master. See. (*Maw, dripping blood.*)

AGRICOLA (*quiet*). Alleluia.

LITORIUS. It tasted so sweet, I thought I should bring some home to share with my wife. Only she don't know where I be.

CAMBYSES. Ay brother. And if you throw up in her sight, be sure you puke up no baby's fingers!

Laughter of them, eerie. The FOURTH WOLF *does not laugh.*

THE OTHERS. Master . . . Master . . .

CAMBYSES. Enough. Enough for now. All have done God's Law.

ALL. Ehmen. Ehmen.

CAMBYSES. Night's near over. Soon be day.

AGNES. Master. Sad . . .

CAMBYSES. Ay. Sad. But we must sleep. Good daughters and good sons, more nights shall come. God's Work is never finished. Sleep for now. Sleep. Sink, easy, in the dewy grass. Roll, in the dew. Wash wolf away. Forget.

The FOURTH WOLF *speaks.*

FOURTH WOLF. It tickles. Master . . . ? Why do it tickle when I go asleepy? Tickles me all over . . .

CAMBYSES. We are not of one skin, as mere men are. We have wolfhairs, that by day grow inward. Dusk, and I call you, out they come growing. Soon the dawn now. Wolvehairs in again. That's the tickle.

Easy. Sleep, wolves. All hearing, scent, and seeing, fade from you. Ay. Shiver. Sniff out your pile of clothes where each had marked it. Stand, severed from the night. Bald, pale, and on

four legs no more. Hurry to your human bed. Do not wake
till you be lying there. Quick. Daybreak. Scatter. I love you
all.

The FOURTH WOLF *remaining.*

CAMBYSES. Lag brother? Wolf still? Hurry! It is nearly day!

FOURTH WOLF. Master . . . My side . . . Down Crooked Glen,
some Briton threw a' axe at me. Its flinthead flew from its
handle as it came. Master . . . ? Master . . . ! My Lord
Cambyses! My side . . . The flinthead . . . is lodged in my side,
sir . . . Master, where are Thou? Lord Cambyses hear Thy
son . . .

Gone. The wounded limp alone. Drag, fast as I can. Hark that!
Cock-a-roo, cock-a-roo! Oh hurry. Else sunlight'll show my
empty bed . . .

I washed in the dew. Rolled wolf away. But not the stone
away. Blind, deaf, slow man again. And lame too now. The
stone's still here. Cock-a-roo cock-a-roo! Hurry to my bed!
Fall to my bed. Hope sleep shall heal me.

Scene Two

Morning. MOTHER ATHDARK *coming with a wooden bucket.*

MOTHER ATHDARK. Athdark. Athdark son. Wake up lad. Day.

ATHDARK *lies curled up like a child beneath skins on a
pallet. (The floor would be strewn with bracken and moss.)*

MOTHER ATHDARK. Athdark. Wake. Till your feet boy. Up.
It's day this long time. Use well the light of the Sun.

Stand lad. Put on ye. Your better clothes. Lord's Day. These
smell of piss. Menfolk and their habits. Hurry. I must milk
that goat out. Udder bain't right. Kids be suckling from 'one
side only. Hurry boy!

ATHDARK (*all early middle age of him*).

I thank Thee Lord that while I slept
safely Thou my soul have kept.

Guard me through the coming day,
and guide me ever in Thy Way.

Ehmen. (*Moves* −)

What's here? This damp on my side . . . Blood . . . ?
Wound . . . ?! Some beast have bit me in the night. In my sleep
and I not wake? I'm not yet wake. Ay. Dreamwound this. I'll
stand, I'll wake, there'll be no wound.

God ha' mercy. I wake and know it. The pain. This wound is
here. How shall I stand to my feet? What shall I do?
Mo (ther) − No. No one must see. 'Athdark? How be ye come
by that hurt?' And I can't answer? Cover. Cover . . .

There's more yet. Like a great rock. Stranger in my body. Egg
of stone, like flinthead of a' axe . . . God my Father! Why do
Thou lodge this here? Chastizing me? Some sin I done? Sin?
Good Christian man. Athdark, of Grimsteads Farm. Good
Christian Roman British Saxon man. No harm to any. No lust
neither. No. Whiter than the snow.

It is the Devil must have done this. Ay. The Devil. To bow me.
To fright me. Mock me. Bow me. I'll not be bowed. Athdark,
up. I'll be not bowed. See, Devil, how I master you?

Put on me. How these clothes shall chafe this wound . . .
Endure. Like 'Spartan boy in 'story. 'I've stole no fox!' Lie.
While fox beneath my coat gnaw all my heart away: stand.
Endure. Betray no pain. I'll master this.

MOTHER ATHDARK (*off*). Athdark!

ATHDARK. No limping neither. Walk. Upright. Stand.

Scene Three

Day. Cold. The Pastor AGRICOLA. *A small congregation:*
AGNES *his wife; a bowed* OLD FARMER; *a woman in black,*
WIDOW FLAX; ATHDARK; MOTHER ATHDARK; LITORIUS,
a comfortable well-dressed Romano-British squire. With a coulter,
AGRICOLA *scores a cross in the hard ground.*

AGRICOLA. Let us bless this new land we have won for our
    plough. *Novam hanc arabilem, in Nomine Domini, et Filii, et*

Spiritus Sancti, ad usum hominum dedicamus. Amen.

ALL. Eh-men. Ehmen.

AGRICOLA. Let us sit.

The community sit, dutiful like children, backs upright —
ATHDARK *particularly, denying his pain. The Pastor*
AGRICOLA *speaks quietly:*

AGRICOLA. Brothers and Sisters in Jesus. From our new book,
God's Word, I tell another story.

Once there was a King. His name was Ahab. His was a hot
country. Hard for us to imagine, in these high cold hills of
Northern Britain; but Ahab's was a land scorched barren by
the Sun. Sand, and rock, that burned the feet to tread on.
Very little grew. King Ahab one day looked out of his palace
window, and saw a goodly garden that his neighbour had,
a poor man. In that scorched and barren kingdom, one little
plot of land, fertile and green, and growing the crops and fruit
of the earth. 'That,' said the King, 'looks just the place for me
to have a pleasure garden. The work's been done, the soil's
been broken. I'll have my men plant flowers there, and
fragrant herbs, to pleasure myself and my queen in the heat
of the day.'

The garden belonged to a man called Naboth. No, said Naboth.
'I'll give you a better garden,' the King said, 'somewhere else.'
No, said Naboth. 'I'll pay you money.' Sir, said Naboth, this
garden was my father's, and my father's father's. When they
came here, they found wilderness. They broke at the rock.
They clove, they cleared; they ploughed, they tilled, they
planted and they watered. I, mile upon mile myself Sir, in this
scorching heat, have carried pails of water on a yoke across my
back. I have husbanded this garden, this work of my fathers;
to hand on down to my sons that follow. It is my heritage, and
it is not mine to give.

The King did not like to be thwarted. He took to his bed. In
a strunt, he turned his face to the wall, and would not eat.
Ah, yous might say, as well they'd let him starve. A King like
that. Only his wife . . . Jezebel . . . A painted woman . . . Said

'Husband, leave this obdurate man to me. You'll have your garden.'

Lo and behind soon after, that poor Naboth found himself up before the courts. On a grave charge. Cursing God. For which the punishment would be stoning unto death. And two strange men he'd never seen till now stood up before the Judge, one then the other, and each swore blind that he'd heard Naboth cursing God. Which they'd never: but theirs was two men's word, and the Judge believed them. Naboth was taken out beyond the village there, and everyone threw stones at him, for cursing God, which he had not done: till his flesh and body were all broken, and he died.

Brothers. Sisters. In this Year of Our Redeemer four hundred and six: in this tenth year of our Beloved Emperor, Honorius, whom God protect —

ALL. Ehmen. Ehmen . . .

AGRICOLA. . . . . High in these cold windscourged hills of Northern Britain have we our garden. East, the length of that bleak shore. North, beneath this mighty Roman Wall, the northern limit of the world. West, to Solway and the sea. Our heritage. THEY, that were here before us, had done nothing. THEY had not broken this hard high land. THEY had not tilled nor sown, nor wrought, nor husbanded, as we. Yet THEY, in their slums and hovels of Turfmires, Pigsty Valley and Crooked Glen, look out like Ahab upon our garden we have made, and smoulder in their hearts. 'Oh,' says Jezebel, 'the land was THEIRS to start with.' Whose was any land, 'to start with'? The beasts'! And forest was its first estate. Is that God's Law, that we must all remain in first estate? Are we to lie on our backs, waiting for God's Grace alone to feed us? God gave me hands. By Will, I raise myself above the beasts. By Will, I rise from first estate. By Will, I break the rock and make a garden. By God's Grace, that garden grows.

Here is the coulter of a plough. The field is God's gift. Her soil, her depth, her fruitful power, are God's Grace. Will, is this iron coulter, by which a furrow may be cut we had not cut till now; and thus God's Grace increased.

Brothers. Sisters. Yet we stand three times a stranger in our garden. We are Romans. We are Saxons. We are British. We are all, yet none of these. We are Roman, by covenant with Rome. Yet southward, along all that road to Rome, her order crumbles. In Rome herself there is worm at the heart. City terrorized, and Emperor fled. We are Romans, and there is no Rome. We are Saxons, by stock. Set here by Rome. All that bleak coast, its signal towers and defences, Rome has named after us. *Litus Saxonicum*: her Saxon Shore. That coast is pounded and plundered now, by others descended from our ancient blood, marauding after. And they'll acknowledge us no kindred when they come. We are Saxons, and Saxons no more. We are British, by land, by dwelling, and by husbandry. Yet THEY, around us and amongst us, those older, darker British, scowl and mutter, hating us to death. How else, indeed? So we are British; but not to THESE.

Be glad. We have a goodly garden. And it is not ours to give. Long ago, Rome brought our fathers here; when she was strong. Gave us her covenant; when she was strong. Now Rome might weary. We do not. No worm is at our heart. Gaul's light goes out. Spain, Danube, Africa. Our light does not go out. Boy-Emperor Honorius, fen-bound in your tower at Ravenna, look out at the night of your world. Your Apennines are dark. Your Alps are dark. Your Rhine is dark. This Wall is not. Here on this Wall alone the flame burns steady. Here alone Honorius is still Emperor. When each of us takes turn to stand on duty on that Wall, Honorius is here. And in our hands is the light of the earth. In ours alone. From that light, Thames, Rhine, Alp, Apennine shall blaze again. The worm at Rome's heart shall die; Rome stand again; and all be restored: from this last living flame we carry. Shield it well, and we shall never be forsaken.

May God now bless this giving of His Word. Let us pray.

All stand.

Scene Four

Day. ATHDARK *huddles from the weather, polishing his Roman helmet.*

ATHDARK. Gal-e-a, eh helmet. Gal-e-ah, oh helmet! Gal-e-am, I do something to a helmet. Gal-e . . . Ga- . . . GaleA galeAH galeAM, ga- . . .

Roman children must be very clever.

Fundus a farmstead. Ager, an acre, rup-es a crag . . .

Is it a little healed? A little nearer coming free . . . ? Try . . . Ease . . .

No. Body must drop this of itself. When?! Daren't turn in my sleep. Can't sleep. This pain. And my dread. I lie, waking. How be I come by this? Why? Stone head in my side . . . ? I walked certain in this world, till now. That God my Father is good to me. Then I wake with this, one Sabbath morning. Why?

The Legion. Eight men one tent. Ten tents one century. Six centuries one cohort, ten cohorts one legion . . . Oh this wound . . .

The Auxiliary Squadron. Thirty-two men one . . . Started again. Wet there at my side. The blood . . . Ah, ah . . . God have mercy. Jesu pity me . . . My skin . . . It stings me all over. It itches me, it crawls . . . What is happening in me . . . ?!

MOTHER ATHDARK (*off*). Athdark?

ATHDARK. Mother not see. No one see . . . Cover cover . . . Lope away, lope away . . .

MOTHER ATHDARK (*coming*). Skulking in the pigsty lad? Athdark? Where'd he go?

WIDOW FLAX (*come with her*). He were limpin'. Did tha remark? Like rabbit had caught paw in a snare. Ah. Don't chivvy the lad. I'll go ma-sen.

MOTHER ATHDARK. Tha will not! A wuiden send a dog out in this filthy weather, let Athdark go. ATHDARK! Great nubbock, you, come here!

ATHDARK (*reappears, normal, bringing rest of Roman uniform*).
Mother?

MOTHER ATHDARK. Run off when I call? Run off when I
call?! I'll fetch ye a clout on yer lug lad! I'll have ye yer
britches down. Widow Flax's goat's broke loose.

WIDOW FLAX. Fretting after they billykids of hers. I parted
they from her too soon. I don't like to hinder, but she's took
off up hillside, both heels of her like the wind . . .

ATHDARK. I've to polish my uniform Mother . . .

MOTHER ATHDARK. She'll be up crags if you don't hurry.

WIDOW FLAX. I don't like to hinder, but she have to be milked.
If she go more nor twelve hour without milking . . .

ATHDARK. Her udder'll split, I know, I know. (*Drops uniform.*)

WIDOW FLAX. You'll hear her bell.

MOTHER ATHDARK. Tha's limpin' lad, why?

ATHDARK. Nowt. Nowt mother. A bruise. Nothing.

Gone.

WIDOW FLAX. Tha's very kind Mother Athdark.

MOTHER ATHDARK. Nay. It's Christian neighbourwork. Come
back down home, Widow Flax, and shut the door. Give churn
a whisk and sit by us' fire. Till Athdark find that goat and
bring her. Oh, this wind . . .

Scene Five

Day. High land. ATHDARK *alone.*

ATHDARK. Nanny Nanny! Nanny Nanny Nanny! Oh this cold.
There's snow on this keen wind. Oh this pain . . . My
wound . . . Seeps blood and . . . and . . . And I itch and
crawl . . . I had to do my uniform. God damn Widow Flax's
goat! Phwwwy phwwy tik tik tik . . . Tch tch tch tch . . . What
was that?! This light . . . Why does this daylight hurt my eyes?
The land's going dark . . . Tik tik tik . . . Tch tch . . . Nanny
Nanny? I jumped then. How did I lep so far so easy? Oh my

pain . . . ! Bite at my pain! Jaws . . . Teeth . . . Bare my mouth
back from my teeth, and bite at my side . . . ! Bend, bend, bite
at my side and punish my pain . . . !

Goatbell somewhere near.

Sh. Easy. Easy . . . No sound . . . Feet, four on the ground . . .
And down of the wind . . .

Gone.

Scene Six

Within. Firelight. MOTHER ATHDARK, WIDOW FLAX *toast
their shins, chewing on bones.*

WIDOW FLAX. Night, and he not home. Ee I'm sorry I put ye
to this trouble.

MOTHER ATHDARK. He'll be home.

WIDOW FLAX. This be a partridge and a half. A while since A
clashed ma teeth in one o' these. Right savoury.

I see no woman, Mother Athdark. Between you and this fire.

MOTHER ATHDARK. What's that?

WIDOW FLAX. Your son. A wife. Tha'll not be here for ever.
Farm needs that other pair of hands. And daughters, and sons.
Able. Afore the father be too old. Also. Your son. He has the
body of a man. That has appetites.

MOTHER ATHDARK. I don't know . . .

WIDOW FLAX. I know. I see him sneak home. Of a daybreak,
once or twice. Reckon some woman down below. While her
husband's on guard up on 'Wall. It has that pattern.

MOTHER ATHDARK. You say that? Another man's wife? That's
never right. There's no land coming with another man's wife.

WIDOW FLAX. If I were that bit younger. And able still to
bear . . .

MOTHER ATHDARK. Mother Flax . . .

WIDOW FLAX. You have to give mind to these things. There's
daughters below.

MOTHER ATHDARK. Who'll marry my son? Who would? Child growed stale, in husk of a man. Never a smile. Athdark is my cross.

WIDOW FLAX. Nights are black. Blanket warms a couple. It's acres wed. Anypath, what is a man? Doltish as a horse. Give him his oats a while, he'll drudge till he drops. It's nature.

MOTHER ATHDARK. Who'd marry Grimsteads? Front line, up here. Wall, three fields away.

WIDOW FLAX. What shall happen? When thou be called aside?

MOTHER ATHDARK. I don't think about it Widow Flax. I daren't die. Athdark? That you?

ATHDARK (*come with bloodied remains of goat across his arms, her bell clanking still*). I'm sorry.

MOTHER ATHDARK. Oh sister . . .

WIDOW FLAX. Am I seeing right?

ATHDARK. I'm sorry to bring the bad word.

WIDOW FLAX. Damn my haste for takin' 'kids from her too early. She were all I had.

MOTHER ATHDARK. That's nature too.

ATHDARK. Ay Mother. Wolf — I must bury this for ye . . .

MOTHER ATHDARK. Tha can rear another. We've two she-kids coming up.

WIDOW FLAX. I couldn't ask . . .

MOTHER ATHDARK. We'll give tha the one.

ATHDARK. We must.

WIDOW FLAX. Well . . .

ATHDARK. Wolf is here. Mother? Wolf have crossed south of the Wall.

MOTHER ATHDARK. Wolf? Wall? What's wall to a wolf? British or Saxon goat's all goat to a wolf, daft son. Bury it boy. — I'll see thee home.

ATHDARK (*remains*). I were man till now. Thought I were. I

were asleep. Dreamed I were a man, like others. Up there I
wake. In sunset, on the crags. Raw goatflesh in my mouth.
Goathide, shredded in my claws. Myself I'm hair all over. Pale,
shite colour. And I'm seeing, on my shadow in the bloodred
sun, my little pointed ears. Oh . . . I am of that company I've
heard of. Those not of one skin. Man outward, wolf inside,
that sink from Man to lope, four feet on the earth, and talk
with the stars, and go wolf-journey. I am. I am. Were-wolf . . .
Joking Father! To give me life, while shaping me not fit to
live! Oh it is worse than my pain. Worse, worse, worse than
pain of the body, oh it is! I must hide somewhere alone, and
think on what I am . . .

MOTHER ATHDARK (*returned*). Not let it prey on thee lad. A
goat's a goat. Wolf is wolf.

If you could only smile. A woman might slip her hand in your
hand. Wife of your own.

ATHDARK. Mother?

MOTHER ATHDARK. You've your tos and froings of a night.
Don't you, son? There's a murk about a man. When
somewhere he's been. Some company. Doings. Not to be
spoken of.

ATHDARK. Mother?

MOTHER ATHDARK. Don't forget lad, I were married to a man.

ATHDARK (*aside*). Inheritance . . . ?

MOTHER ATHDARK. What's that? Och son. Learn to smile.
Deserve a good woman. Bury that, and then some supper.

ATHDARK. Don't want supper! . . .

MOTHER ATHDARK. Away to your bed then after. Bury that.
I'll wake till I hear ye come in. Good night. God watch ye son.

ATHDARK (*remains*). Is it still true? It is still true. I am. I am . . .
that. (*Takes up the items of his uniform.*) Oh gal-e-a, I am
unworthy. Lorica squamata, 'breastplate with fishscales', I soil
you from within. My wolfskin smirches you. Spatha my
sword, oh hasta, pallium, not worthy . . .

No. Dry my eyes. I see now. God is good. He sent me this stone and wound to show me what I am. These are His Grace, they waken me. I've seen now how I came by these. Well then I'll master that. By Will. Bury this, it's past and done. I shall be wolf no more.

Goes with carcase.

ACT TWO

Scene One

A grove of trees, hung with gently tinkling offerings. A young priestess, CEIRIAD, *in virginal white.*

CEIRIAD. Lady. Lady. Lady of Mercy, Lady of Healing, Lady of Grief. I always have to bring before You the prayers of others, and never speak to You of what I need or I desire.

Women and girls come here to Your high dwelling, with little images in clay, of hands or feet that are hurt, of eyes, ears, organs that pain or fail them. They place them all about Your sacred trees, for the touch of Your restoring mercy. I intercede with You for that. It is my office.

There's something else. Some of the girls bring little clay hearts — not hearts of theirs, but of men. Men: they seek to turn toward them. Sometimes the image is of something grosser than a heart, something of a man I've never seen. I've never seen a man. The girls whisper and giggle about all this. They say it's for something called Love. I am Your priestess, they say, and I would not know of this Love. Lady, don't be angry. Lady, smile on me. Lady, You are virgin, You understand. I bring You . . . I bring You a little clay heart I've made . . . Who's that? who's there? Lady? Lady are You still here? The heart of a man I don't know, nor even who he is. That somewhere his heart turn to me, and I know Love.

If I make You angry, Lady, I'm sorry. If I am never to know Love at all, then, Lady, help me more, to be alone.

An older priestess, SULGWEN, *has come. She is in white and green.*

SULGWEN. Ceiriad? Ceiriad girl? Leave Our Lady be. She has Her work cut out, healing all these pains and broken hearts. You've interceded long enough.

CEIRIAD. We say She heals. We do the healing . . .

SULGWEN. Hers is the Grace. Ours are the hands. What's that? A heart? You girl? Heart? Whose? A man? what man? You don't know any man.

CEIRIAD. Just a man.

SULGWEN. Oh girl, girl . . . Girl, girl . . .

CEIRIAD. What's wrong with wanting Love?

SULGWEN. You're a priestess.

CEIRIAD. It could have been worse. It could have been one of those . . . things of a man.

SULGWEN. Ay. Well. That was never much. Oh girl, girl, leave it be. Leave Our Lady to Her work. It's sunset, we must tidy the shrine. And don't you stand there, looking southward for a man. Wall down there, end of the world is that. Nothing good came up from south of it.

CEIRIAD. I don't want to live my life alone.

SULGWEN. You can love, and be alone. Oh yes. Anypath . . .

CEIRIAD. What?

SULGWEN. Nothing.

CEIRIAD. You were going to tell me something.

SULGWEN. Was I?

CEIRIAD. Yes.

SULGWEN. Perhaps I was. Perhaps I'm not. Help me.

CEIRIAD. Sulgwen. Am I to be a priestess all my life?

SULGWEN. Why not?

CEIRIAD. You weren't. You came here from the world.

SULGWEN. Oh, the world . . .

CEIRIAD. All I know I know from you. Sulgwen?

SULGWEN. What?

CEIRIAD. I had a father.

SULGWEN. Of course you had. That's all you need to know for now.

CEIRIAD. For now? Who was he?

SULGWEN (*silence*).

CEIRIAD. Tell me.

SULGWEN (*silence*).

CEIRIAD. Why, what shall that do to me? When I know. It shall frighten me? Or make me sad? Who am I?

SULGWEN. Lady. Know that, and you are in the world indeed.

CEIRIAD. You call me Lady.

SULGWEN. Yes. Start you down the path home. Yes. I'll tell you. Start down the path. I'll close the shrine.

(*Alone*). All my days here, I have dreaded this.

Follows after.

Scene Two

Night. The wall. A ROMAN NCO.

NCO. Milecastle Forty-Two. Arsehole of the Universe. Oh these nights. Jupiter send me a posting in the Sun. Who goes there?

ATHDARK (*off*). Amicus.

NCO. What? Oh. You. Athkard. Kind of you to show up. Guardmount was at midnight but no matter. Your mates have been on this wall two hours. Pastor. Old man. No matter. Clank clank clank. *Iesus Hominum Salvator,* the rubbish I get sent. Athkart, what is this?

ATHDARK. L- lo- lor- squ-

NCO. What?

ATHDARK. L-lorica squamata Corporal —

NCO. Breastplate with fishscales, I can see. This gap you twit. Call this protection do you against the heathen arrows? You could drive a socking great baggage-train from Colchester to York through this. It's horrible. It's like the goddess Sul-Minerva's horrible great oozing mouth, I hate it. Dress yourself in proper order! And stand up straight! Where is your sword?

ATHDARK. Spathum, spathum . . . Oh. Sword . . . Oblitus . . .

NCO. Forgot it. Forgot your sword. Item: wall: Roman: one: limestone: Hadrian's: Northern Front for the defence of: length: Wallsend-on-Tyne to Bowness-on-Solway, eighty miles: thickness, eight foot, height twelve foot including forward parapet: the whole, when fully operational, which at this moment it alas is not, deploying on average one man per sixty-seven paces: and you forget your sword. No matter. No matter. To your post! Move!

Oh these nights. Milecastle Forty-Two. Hadrian's Wall. Britannia Inferior. The Empire. The World. The Universe. Space . . . Space. Earth. Britannia. Wall. Sweet Forty-Two. Anus of the cosmos. All fetch up here. The dregs. The slops. Wogs from Egypt. Syrian archers. Sausage-benders from the Danube. Least they were soldiers. Your lot: 'Defence Regiment: Part time'. See these? Athkrat?

ATHDARK. I- in- scr- ipt-

NCO. Inscriptions yeah. See what these say? Legions. Twentieth Valeria Victrix. Second Augusta. That was an army.

ATHDARK. La-ti-nam litter-as . . .

NCO. What?

ATHDARK. La-ti-nam —

NCO. Know what you are? Aftercart? A barbaros. People who can only say Bar bar. Oh get down off the Roman Wall! Down! Stand facing South and terrify your own! *Iesus H Salvator,* the rubbish — And straighten your helmet!

ATHDARK. Galea . . . Galea . . .

NCO. Bar bar! Roll on death. (*Moves away.*)

ATHDARK. I don't speak Latin very well. Gal-e-a gal-e-a gal-e-am . . . G- ga- Gal-e-ae gal-e-ae gal-e-AH! Of a helmet, to or for a helmet, by with or from a helmet! I've got it! Gal-e- . . . I SHALL prevail — !

NCO. Why you keep scratching your head? You growing horns? There's heads in this world have horns, if we but knew it.

Rather not know. Come down off duty early of a dawn. Find our wife, legs up around some great Brit's back. And I'm on this wall. Last honest man in the world, I sometimes feel. Before that dark.

ATHDARK. Ug. Ug. S- si- signa-

NCO. What?

ATHDARK. Sig-na-li-a . . .

NCO. Where? Ah. Signaltower. Him. Joker. Not important.

ATHDARK. Mul. Ce . . .

NCO. He was at that earlier. Wants his parts caressed. Leave him.

ATHDARK. Mi. Hi . . .

NCO. You can't read. Yet pick up Latin semaphores. Army education. Does wonders for a man. 'Parts'. Wouldn't know about those would you? Think they're for stirring your porridge. As well. Get burned at the stake for touching those now. New Christian laws. Come back Jupiter, all is forgiven.

ATHDARK. Mul. Ge . . .

NCO. Not important.

ATHDARK. Mi. Hi . . .

NCO. Nothing. Signalia — nil! Right. Krautfeatures. I leave you on your jack a while. Look in on your friends. Pastor. Old man . . . You stay here. Guard Wall alone. See? He's given over. Stand. Here. Alone. Hope to Christ your sword's not called for. It's a quiet night. So long. Daftark. Rome's last hope. My stripes weep.

ATHDARK (*alone*). Solum he said. Alone. I watch the Wall alone. Defend my Emperor. 'Who's that? Who's there?'

Silence.

ATHDARK. Brit . . . Brit . . . The name's a dread. Since I were a child. All his names. Welshman. Cumri . . . Come in child, or the Welshman'll get thee. Don't go down Cumri town. Don't stray west of Grindon Lough. Brit land. Bad land. Brit, Welsh, Cumri, I've dreamed of them, creeping at dusk like vampires from their graves. To fire our farms, kill victims of us they have chosen, stone by stone tak' Roman bridge apart. Not heard. Not seen. Shapes of night, that melt into the daybreak. Only their havoc showing they had been. 'They were over last night. Those ones.' Welsh. Brit. Cumri . . . And nowt of vampire I might see about him. Bastard, that can't be told from a man!

Who's there?! Who's out there in the dark . . . ?

Scene Three

MOTHER ATHDARK, WIDOW FLAX *watch tumult obscurely heard below.*

MOTHER ATHDARK. Burning our town. Broad daylight now. The savages. Come out from their holes in the ground. Turfmire. Pigsty Valley. Beggarbogs. And fire our goodly garden of a town.

WIDOW FLAX. There's Lawcourts gone. Bathhouse look. It'll be they granaries next. Ee, those'll burn. It's three-sixty-seven all over again. That were a year for Devil's vintages.

MOTHER ATHDARK. Hark at them. Chanting their rebel incantations. Bar bar . . . Wattin' at their heathen gongs. Well for Rome. Dumpin' us here. Front line: then tie one hand behind our backs. We should have had powers to kill 'em all. Go into Beggarbogs and grub 'em out, root stock and branch. The only answer.

WIDOW FLAX. There's Monument gone! Tippin and wavin. To his knees . . . Weeeeeeeh! Flat on his face.

MOTHER ATHDARK. That were a general of ours on that. In sixty-seven he held that town.

WIDOW FLAX. Ee, destruction. You have to hand it to they buggers. They knows how to wreck a place. Here come 'soldiers. Like goatshites off a shovel. Kilts awaftin. Hey laddie, show us a blick o thy arse! WeeeeYEH! That takes me back.

MOTHER ATHDARK. Widow Flax.

WIDOW FLAX. Arse: best part on a man. There's York Street afire . . . !

MOTHER ATHDARK. Brit bastards. Welsh, Cumri, whatever ye's call your shitey-hearted selves. Why can't ye fight straight? Straight. Don't know the meaning of the word. Did ever a Brit look tha straight in the eye? Can't even shite straight. Jezebel! Ahab! Wi your skelly eyes and corkscrew arseholes! *Civis Romanus Sum!*

Explosion.

MOTHER ATHDARK. They'd only to wait. Ay. I knowed a British man. He had Britishman's Disease. Couldn't work. 'Oh me back . . .' Couldn't build a hedge nor help wi a plough. 'Me back . . .' He could breed though.

WIDOW FLAX. Oh ay, he saw to that all right.

MOTHER ATHDARK. All day, moanin and groanin. 'Oh woman, me back . . .' His brood all about him. Bow legs, snattery noses, little runny piggy eyes. His back were wondrous supple where it came to conjugation.

Explosion nearer. WIDOW FLAX *flees.*

MOTHER ATHDARK. You'd only to wait! Your over-breedin' 'ud have swamped us all!

And my one son . . .

Scene Four

High. ATHDARK *shivering.*

ATHDARK. 'Fetch widow watter.' 'Not from near spring, Athdark lad, I seen a dog there cock his leg.' 'Ay son, from farther spring. For Widow Flax. Up stream.' Fetch widow watter. Fetch widow hay fetch widow straw. Find widow goat, prune widow apple tree, fetch widow watter. Piss in her watter, sod her goat!

My pain . . . My pain . . . !!

What lacked Athdark ever from being a man? Don't know. Something. No matter now. Too late. This wound. This stone this wound. Never heal now . . . Oh my side, my side, oh my side . . . !

What is that earth outside of me? New moss, the colour of piss on snow . . . Cold grey ashrood. Buds, black, shaped like knob of a little boy . . . Bent, shivering thorn . . . Shiver like Athdark, shake, shake . . . Dead leaves clatter, clack clack clack . . . Dried like Athdark . . . Oh my pain . . . Lark there, do bob and lift and spill her song. Outside this pain . . . !

High here . . . How am I come so high? Rigg yonder . . . Crag . . . Where's this I am? Rigg, crag . . . Snout. Scar . . . Have I crossed that wall there and not known it? Sweet scent burning. Turf . . . ? Bad land? Brit country? Wall be broken . . . Mother . . . ?! Hurry . . . Hurry lad, home . . . Up, up . . . Over . . . The world's turned round about me, the Sun at my back is in the North . . . Hurry! Hurry! Oh my pain . . . I am all fire. Tear off my skin! This light! Tear out my eyes! This roaring in my head . . . Tear off my head . . . ! Tear up the earth! Tear down the Sun . . . ! Mother . . . !

CEIRIAD *appears beyond.* ATHDARK *falls.*

CEIRIAD. Dinio? Dinio? (*She calls off:*) Sulgwen, a Hulgwen! — Dinio?

ATHDARK. What? Who are — (*Loses consciousness.*)

SULGWEN (*comes*). Howling flailing thrashing seething. A beast, that. Fling him back over. Soon your father will be coming.

CEIRIAD. No! Is wounded he is. Look. Blood from his side. In the wound, look. A stone. We must heal this.

SULGWEN. Fling him back over his wall.

CEIRIAD. We are sisters in Our Lady's Mercy.

SULGWEN. Not to him we're not. This sullies Her. See you the clothing is on him. Saxon is this.

CEIRIAD. Oh Hulgwen Hulgwen, Saxon is a word. This looks more like a man. I command you. Since now I may.

SULGWEN. Ay Lady. Now you may. So must you remember now. This is your Kingdom's enemy.

CEIRIAD. My father's enemy.

SULGWEN. Your father is dying. Soon you inherit. The struggle. And the enemy. It was easy before. A banished priestess in that shrine: all you must do, Our Lady's simple will. To comfort and to heal. Soon you are Queen. Of Lost Britain. Heal him, you heal the thief of your Kingdom. This does not know Our Lady. This does not recognize Her Grace.

CEIRIAD. She is yet his Lady. He is Hers. Help me bring him.

SULGWEN. If you say . . .

A funeral drum.

CEIRIAD. They are here . . . ? Already . . . ? Oh we have to hide him . . . In this cleft in the rock . . . Till we can bring him out and heal him . . . Sulgwen help me . . . ! Gently . . . Oh . . . Oh they are here . . .

A process in black. A young Celt, LUGOVELIN.

LUGOVELIN. Is this the shrine of Saitada, Our Lady of Grief?

SULGWEN. Sir? It is.

LUGOVELIN. Where is the Priestess, Sulgwen?

SULGWEN. Here am I.

LUGOVELIN. I bring a daughter her father, his last road home.

SULGWEN. Your Queen is ready.

CEIRIAD. Cousin?

LUGOVELIN. Lady.

CEIRIAD. You are my cousin. Lugovelin. You stayed at my father's side, when my sisters cast him out into the storm. Good Lugovelin. Oh let me see him . . .

The OLD KING *is discovered, of grey wild head, and borne upright, dead, upon the throne.*

LUGOVELIN. We had hoped he might live. To speak some words with you. At least, to see you . . .

CEIRIAD. Father . . . ?

LUGOVELIN. Something he saw. Something . . . We bore him

south, toward the frontier. Lammermuir, Teviot . . . We rested
neither night nor day. We came to these Border hills. He was
asleep. We breasted the watershed at Carter Bar. There he
might see. We paused there. We waited. For him to waken.
If he might waken: at the scent and sounds of his own land,
lost so long. There were primrose on the mountain. A curlew's
crying. In the pale gold Sun, from the white crusts of the
hills below, a touch of warm light, and the chill of snow. He
wakened. We raised him a little. Supported him. Facing, out,
above his promised Kingdom. He tried to speak. To point.
Something he saw. He said: 'Look there . . . Look there . . .'

CEIRIAD. Father? Father . . .

She cradles the grey head, crooning a wordless song:

We must enthrone him in the tomb. Cousin? Facing South,
toward the land.

LUGOVELIN, *procession pass.*

SULGWEN. Winding is the road indeed, and blind, by which
you come to what is yours from the beginning. And a prayer
is answered.

CEIRIAD. What prayer?

SULGWEN. Think. Crown. Lost Britain, yet to be rewon. The
struggle. Now in these hands. You have your prayer. You are
virgin to the world no more. That Saxon man. I'll mend his
wound, and have him taken back. Here's Lugovelin. Listen
to him.

LUGOVELIN (*cautiously returned*). Cousin? Sister? Ceiriad?
Your father . . . This was not Llyr coming home to Britain.
Britain there, is coming home to him. Exile's long night is all
but done. We gather south, toward the day. Rome is soon
gone. We watch her, as the crows watch a sheep that's dying
on the hillside. We watch for that . . . stillness . . . Then we . . .
Oh then the Kingdom. Lost to us so long. Comes to fall, into
our hands. In our time. In your hands. Our hands.
Together . . . (?)

She has withdrawn from him.

Scene Five

Amid tinkling trees. Image of a goddess. ATHDARK *awakes.*
(The wound is healed.)

ATHDARK. I float in the air. So easy. I am dead. Ascended
into Heaven. I like it. So. God's Garden. Paradise. Like trees.
Trees of Heaven. Where be Jesus? Strange . . . Paradise: and
after THEIR religion . . . Pagan images. We've been wrong . . .

He sleeps again. CEIRIAD *and* SULGWEN *come.*

SULGWEN. He's sleeping. The wound will heal now. Soon we
must find a way to take him back.

CEIRIAD. Yes. Yes . . .

ATHDARK (*waking*). Voices of angels . . . Ladies of angels . . .
Lovely and bright . . . Angels . . .

CEIRIAD. What's he saying? Anghelen, it sounded. What is
that? — Sir? Sir?

ATHDARK. Deenio, she calls me.

CEIRIAD. He understands!

ATHDARK. Angel?

CEIRIAD. Anghel he calls me. Is that some Saxonish name?
Who is he thinking I am? — Sir? Sir?

ATHDARK. Deenio? Me? Strange tongue these angels speak.

SULGWEN. Fever is on him still. And on him is no knowing
where he is.

CEIRIAD. Holy ground. Holy ground.

ATHDARK. Ne. Me. Tah . . . ?

CEIRIAD. Holy ground, yes! He understands!

ATHDARK. Ne. Me. Tah . . . I must learn these words of Heaven.

CEIRIAD. We must learn Saxonish.

SULGWEN. Why? We are in our country. Where is he?

ATHDARK. Something was in my side. Now so easy . . . I fell
asleep. I wake in Paradise. And Paradise is after THEIR
religion. Images. Pagan trinkets hanging. Tink tink tink.
Paradise is THEIRS. Yet I'm not damned. Love is here. A
smiling angel.

CEIRIAD: That name again he calls me. Anghel.

ATHDARK. She is!

CEIRIAD. May he stand?

SULGWEN. Let him. Let him walk. Let him fall in that river. One
of his kind the less.

CEIRIAD. A Hulgwen. Where is your healing Grace? Stand
Sir . . . Easy . . .

ATHDARK. The angel touches me. And I don't burn. These
clouds of Heaven . . . they take my weight . . . Or I've no
weight at all. This Heaven's not what 'preacher said. It is called
Ne me ta. Ne me ta. Hope I've said the right thing.

CEIRIAD. He understands. — Yes. Yes! The Grove of Oak Trees!

ATHDARK. Der ou oi . . . Der ou oi . . . Must be Heavenish for
oak. Oaks of Heaven.

CEIRIAD. River. River.

ATHDARK. Ahvona. River. Ahvona. Heaven is fashioned so like
earth! Nay. Earth were in Heaven's image. A lowlier likeness,
of this . . . Paradise . . . These words, though. Deruoi. Ahvona.
Nemeta . . . I have no Heavenish. Shall that bar me at the
Gate?

CEIRIAD. Sir?

ATHDARK. This Deenio she calls me: must be my Heavenish name.

CEIRIAD. Water.

ATHDARK. Gwisca . . . ?

CEIRIAD. Mountain.

ATHDARK. Monidho . . .

CEIRIAD. Walk . . .

ATHDARK. Paths of Heaven! Why did they not teach us this below? (*Moves away.*)

CEIRIAD. His wound is healed.

SULGWEN. I should have more poisoned it. Come away. You must.

Scene Six

MOTHER ATHDARK, *the* OLD FARMER, *Pastor* AGRICOLA *labour to repair the Wall. The Roman-British Squire* LITORIUS *in charge.*

LITORIUS. Come on old man. A little effort. We're mending a breach in the world, you realize. Rome this side, chaos that. Christ here, darkness beyond. Limès, limitis: here values end. That's the spirit old girl,. Remember Hadrian. Let Hadrian be our example. Surveying this frontier, every mile. On foot; bareheaded: wind and weather. Planning this Wall. Its route. Alignment. Height, length, thickness. Spacing of garrisons. Milecastles, signal-towers —

AGRICOLA. Squire Sir? I think she ought to be allowed to (go home . . .)

LITORIUS. What? Watch where you're putting things in, old man! Inscription, that. I don't know. Bung it back in, any old where. Back to front. Text upside-down. 'Soldier . . . D- Dagvald . . .' Hmf. Some German. . . . Lord Almighty, what a botch. Hadrian would turn in his grave. Not the funds he had, of course. Nor the numbers. For all that, this wall still stands. Our Covenant in stone. Our Sovereignty. Our legacy of three centuries. Our Heritage.

. . . Oh look at this damage. Look at this. And those people
out there call themselves a culture? You can almost hear the
land there squirming. With their ill will. Smell it . . . Smell it,
old man, can you? Turf they burn. To warm themselves. Sweet
smell. Dangerous. Incense of rebellion. WottaDEENi.

OLD FARMER. What?

LITORIUS. WottaDEENi. Name of their Seltic tribe.
GoDODDHin they call themselves. Can't even spell their own
name. No writing, of course. Oral culture. Gift of words. Oh
yes. See that, old lady? All that land out there? We gave them
that. Whole new country, all to themselves. Leave 'em alone,
and they'd leave us alone. You'd think. That carnage in our
town last Friday. Women. Children. Innocent soldiers. Horses!
Horrifying, what some people will do. Not only Selts. Look.
Eastward, by the sea. That rhythmic flashing of light, old
man. Clifftop signal-tower. Warning of the approach of suspect
vessels, very like. Saxon marauders. Those towers scan that
North Sea day and night. Defending your rights, old man.
More than your rights. A village where the Saxon's been is not
a pretty sight.

OLD FARMER. We be Saxons.

LITORIUS. What?

AGRICOLA. He says we're Saxons Sir.

LITORIUS. What? Of course you are. But loyal Saxons.

OLD FARMER. We be British too.

LITORIUS. What? Ah, British too. Of course you are. Of course
you are. Saxon British. The best. Rome's most loyal. Our
Emperor says his prayers for you. Every night. 'God bless
especially the Roman British Saxons.'

OLD FARMER. We be not Romans.

LITORIUS. What's that? Not Romans? Well . . . out here how
could you be? But you live by Roman standards. You enjoy
the Roman Peace — Who's this? Looks like a military
gentleman. Hurrying our way. Waving? Take over Parson will
you? He'll want to talk to *me* . . .

OLD FARMER. Pastor can I go? I'm worried about my lambs.

AGRICOLA. I'll talk to him. Leave that. Mother Athdark, leave it be.

MOTHER ATHDARK. I will not. It lets me from worrying. About my son. It lets me from fearing the night to come. Me without him in that farm my lone.

AGRICOLA. I know I know. But you must rest.

MOTHER ATHDARK. I daren't. Daren't rest. Daren't stop . . .

LITORIUS (*returned*). Parson. A word.

Brings AGRICOLA *aside.*

OLD FARMER. He gone? Sod this for a game of soldiers. I'm going to see to my lambs.

MOTHER ATHDARK (*alone*). Oh my poor back. I'm pains all. I'm bad this long time. Oh my back . . . I must home to my bed . . . (*Goes.*)

LITORIUS. Convey no anxiety please. I must hurry and warn my wife. (*Goes.*)

AGRICOLA. How do you tell your people that the unthinkable has happened? News from the mainland, so long reaching us . . . ! Now we hear. Last midwinter, from Cologne to Mainz the Rhine froze over. German tribes began to gather on the further bank. Thousands. Tens of thousands. Tens of tens of thousands. New Year's Eve, they swarmed across the solid ice. Cologne is rubble. Mainz, Trier, Amiens are ashes. The Goth is on his way to Rome.

ACT THREE

Scene One

Night. MOTHER ATHDARK, *sick. The Pastor* AGRICOLA.

MOTHER ATHDARK. Pastor. I have this dream. I'm stood on a
shore. It looks out westward. What shore could that be, ha?
I could be on, that looks out westward. I'm there among a lot
of folk. The tide is coming in. From 'far edge of the world.
Long, low, black flood of it. And the roar of it coming. All
that folk of us start stumbling backwards. Up a slope. The
slope is grassy. Backwards, up, up that grassy slope. The sand
below's all swamped wi' watter. The slope we're on is a rigg, all
hummocks. On each hummock is a house. Our houses. Round,
beehive shäpen. O' wattle and clay, and thatched wi' reeds.
We're all screaming: 'The flood! The flood!' We're earthing our
houses over. We're building another house on top. Smaller,
but higher. But smaller. 'The flood! The flood . . . !'

AGRICOLA. Sh, sh . . . Lie still . . .

MOTHER ATHDARK. Where is my son? With them ones burning
down our farms, you'd think I'd dream of flames, not
watter . . .

AGRICOLA. It's nothing. You dream a dread that once did
happen. Mother Athdark. Long before our time. To all our
folk. And not in one day it happened. Years, years it took.
Along another shore.

MOTHER ATHDARK. Pastor . . . ! What's that . . . ?

AGRICOLA. A German shore. Friesland they call it. Some of
us . . . our forbears . . . that shore was our land. We dwelled
there, on mounds before the sea. In pointed thatch houses just
as you saw. A Roman writer tells us . . . You sleep. Sleep,
sister. God spare you the terror of the dream . . .

Year by year, the tide reached further in. Year by year, it
claimed our shore. We earthed our old houses over, built on

top. The flood rose higher, year by year. Till the knab of each
mound was all of our land that was left. And our . . . last, little
houses . . . Travellers say they see the remains of them.
Beneath the flood . . .

End of Part One

PART TWO

ACT THREE

Scene Two

Day. The tinkling grove. ATHDARK *in wonder like a child.*

ATHDARK. Ne . . . me . . . ta. Ne . . . me . . . ta. I walk on
clouds. I don't fall through. There, below, that mortal wall,
that severs they living from us dead. Yet I feel . . . I feel
myself to be . . . more living than I was . . . Deep in my
side . . . a new stone . . . It beats, like a baby . . . in my . . .
heart . . . ? The lovely angel . . . I have felt in my sleep the
touch of her healing hands . . . There she is. This Heaven's a
wonder. I should have died before.

CEIRIAD, SULGWEN *come, cloaked for a journey.*

CEIRIAD. He walks some other country, in the head. It amazes
him. Oh, how might we bend our brother to this world again?

SULGWEN. Let him go back to his own. To his labours. That'll
bend him to the world.

CEIRIAD. Labour? Suppose he were a king's son?

SULGWEN. Oh . . .

CEIRIAD. Yes. A prince . . .

SULGWEN. In that he came wearing?

CEIRIAD. What did I come wearing, to that shrine? His father
could be angry king, who cast him out, as mine did me. We
cannot see by looking what his clay might hide, that I
should call him brother.

SULGWEN. What might that be?

CEIRIAD. Inheritance. He has his heritage. All have that.
Sulgwen, imagine. Beyond that wall, just so far from it as I
was, here: a son of a king, as I was a daughter, all this while
come stumbling his blind way . . . And I to him . . . Till here
we meet.

SULGWEN. Ay, in a mirror. Glass cracked, the phantom gone, and you with a face streaming blood. You have your prince. His name is Lugovelin. Man of our kind.

CEIRIAD. I don't . . .

SULGWEN. Don't what?

ATHDARK. They come to bring me a journey. Must be to the Throne of God. Was God a Goddess all along? Nothing I learned below has made me ready. I've so much still to master. Gwisca, water . . .

CEIRIAD. Yes, yes! The earth, the earth!

ATHDARK. Teer? Teer? The ground . . . ? No . . . Can't be ground. Not here in Heaven . . .

SULGWEN. This I should have done before. Our Lady of Healing or no. Your will, or no . . .

CEIRIAD. What are you doing?

SULGWEN. Do you want him seeing his way to the Wall? Remembering?

ATHDARK. She comes to cover my eyes. Must be against the Light of God. I come to Judgment.

CEIRIAD. That golden head . . . Lugovelin's is not gold.

SULGWEN. Any man's head can be gold in the dark. It's kingdoms that marry. But not this man's and ours. Forget him. Now.

CEIRIAD. I shall never forget him. He is my first brother. Man to me is him for ever. Oh my heart . . . I feel . . .

SULGWEN. I know what you feel. So let's have done.

CEIRIAD. Not yet! Let me look at him a moment more. Let me be girl a moment longer . . .

SULGWEN. I'll tell you a story, about a girl and a man . . .

CEIRIAD. Sulgwen no! Your stories all end in madness and pain. You would have me afraid to open my eyes for fear the light might blind me.

SULGWEN. Open your eyes is what I want.

CEIRIAD. Let me look at him.

ATHDARK. Strange. I seem the only dead. We die our lone. Angels bring each of us our one blind journey. Till the moment we behold Jerusalem, City of Light. Around me, hosts of the numberless dead throng toward the Throne. Wives, and harlots. Childer that died. Kings in their purple and gold, beggars with sores. Soldiers with their mortal wounds . . . Was I a soldier . . . ?

CEIRIAD. He is a king. I know it.

SULGWEN. Where are you taking him?

CEIRIAD. To the height of my father's tomb. From there he shall see our city Dinas Maros, and know it for a city of kings. The sight shall wake in him the memory of his own blood!

SULGWEN (*cries after*). He is Saxon! Man and Saxon, that's all we know! Even he had king's blood in him, what majesty of ours shall his sight see? Dinas Maros, royal city? Hovels, he'll see! Weems, dug half in the earth! Our beggarhood on this sill of our own land!

Oh . . . Talk to the wind. As well beseech the waters of the mountain lake . . .

Scene Three

High. CEIRIAD *brings* ATHDARK, *removes the blindfold.*

CEIRIAD. Brother. King. Man. Whose name I do not know. Now you have eyes.

ATHDARK. What shall I see? I'm afraid . . . I hear lark and curlew song . . . That's only right. All Creation praises Him. Or Her . . .

CEIRIAD. Look up.

ATHDARK. Eyebright. Primrose. Blossom all about on this green cloud of Heaven. Cowslip, violet, lady's smock . . . Spring flowers . . . Spring. Must be Spring all the time, in . . . Her sight . . . I curse that Pastor. I curse all who taught me below, that God's a Father, and I should feel shame before him. Shame is easy. But this loveliness . . .

CEIRIAD. Look. The world. And our city there. Dinas Maros.

ATHDARK. Jerusalem! Shining city. Oh glorious handiwork
of God. What their Sabbaths must be. Their joy, that sing
around Him all the time, in golden crowns in the City of
Light . . .

CEIRIAD. You hear the music from there? They're making
ready. In that city tonight, the music there'll be. The feasting.
All in my name. Oh how can I tell you? How can I have you
understand? The joy in my kingdom, and none in my heart.

ATHDARK. I am here to be saved. I know it. The glance of
Judgment shall pierce my heart, but I've no fear now —

What's that fragrance? Sweet . . . Scent of . . . of burning . . .
Smell of . . . hatred . . . ? Rebellion . . . ? in Heaven . . . ?

No . . . No . . .

Who's that below me? Old man's soul, bowed to the flat of
the cloud? Working with a spade . . . ? Toil? In Heaven . . . ?
Hagging up from the cloud a brick of mire . . . ?

No . . . No . . .

Heaven? Bog and mire? He's looking up at me. His eyes . . .
From here, it pierces me . . . The hating in his eyes . . .
I'm going to fall . . . I'm falling . . .

CEIRIAD. My love?

ATHDARK. Do not touch me! Oh . . . Athdark, what have I
done? I was never dead? I am man still? Flesh, bone . . . ?
Maimed as I was? No stone in my side. That's somehow gone.
But the pain . . .

CEIRIAD. Brother . . . ?

ATHDARK. Whore of Ahab! Not Heaven. Not Heaven. Cumri
land. Wall again. Living again. Toil again. Pain again. My
lone again. And cold by night . . . Wall . . . ? Wall . . . ?
South, Sun, Wall . . . !

CEIRIAD. No! No! Come back! (*Takes up the blindfold.*) His
eyes were here. I did not dream this . . .

SULGWEN (*come*). It is the dream that woke. And it has left you. Good. Now you wake too.

CEIRIAD. Why must you always be so sound?!

SULGWEN. He hates you now!

CEIRIAD. He is in my heart! That hatred in his eyes, that only burns him deeper, in my heart . . .

SULGWEN. He is nothing. Even if he have the makings of a man. Dry your eyes. Lugovelin is waiting on the road. To bring us to Dinas Maros. As for a man . . . Nights are dark. There can be one man in your bed, and another be the story in your heart. If that's how it has to be. Come down.

Scene Four

Burnt farm. ATHDARK; MOTHER ATHDARK, *dead. Failing day.*

ATHDARK. Mother? Mother speak. You're angry with me, I can see. I've done nothing. Mother? Mother eat. Eat, mother, else you'll die. Tk tk tk, come on. A sup o' this. Sup on it only. Open your mouth. Open. Damn ye, Mother, eat! Ee, you can be a stubborn cow when you've a mind. Eat! Must A feed ye like a bairn now? That how you'll hold on to me?! Look at your face. All dribble.

. . . Those eyes. Accusing me. I been nowhere. Think I'd neglect ye Mother? When did I neglect you? Daren't, Mother. Daren't. Leave you one moment, look what happens. Farm burn down. You think I think you're dead. Don't tha? Think you fool me you be dead. To punish me. Think you frighten me. Make me feel guilty. Wouldn't put it past you Mother. Moment my back be turned. To sit up in your bed and die on me. Carnaptious sow.

Speak. Speak! I'll shake ye! Ee, that stubborn. Lie you down then. Starve if you will. And shut those eyes. Shut, damn ye! Lie face to 'wall. The way I needn't see ye. Accusing with those eyes. I been nowhere. I done nothing. Who's that, who's there? I can hear ye Mother. 'Wait till your father get home!'

'Son? Son?! What have you done with the farm?! What have
you done with Mother lad?' 'Nothing Father, nothing . . .'
Who's that? Who's there . . . ? Father . . . ? Mustn't see. He
mustn't see. I'll dress in Mother's clothes, he'll not notice. In
this light. Till bedtime and his hands come groping . . . Haha!
Who's there?

CAMBYSES (*somewhere unseen*). Athdark?

ATHDARK. Oh . . . The voice of Wrath . . . In the cool of the
day . . . Hide me, hide . . . Where's table gone? Brits took
table. No roof, no walls . . . I be naked under the sky . . .

CAMBYSES (*unseen*). Athdark, where have you been? What
havoc here. Destruction . . . Ill have you husbanded your
garden. They watch from above, bequeathed it ye. Your
garden had need of ye: Athdark, where were you? Were you
a-shitin'? Bad steward of the vine? I see ye. I see ye all the
time. I am your Lord Cambyses, I see all.

ATHDARK. No! No!

CAMBYSES (*dim form ill-seen*). Look boy. On shoulder of yon
fell. The Sun go down. Look. The wolf is eating the Sun.

ATHDARK. No! Sun, stay!

CAMBYSES. The wolf shall eat it all.

ATHDARK. Sun stay with me!

CAMBYSES (*wolfhead, monstrous in the dying light*). The wolf
shall eat it all! Then night is come. For Athdark, night for
ever.

ATHDARK. No! Fathers in Heaven, forgive me! Lord Cambyses,
plead with my fathers!

CAMBYSES. How can you buy back that Sun? Look. Gone.
All in a moment. One last green flare from it, and gone. Dusk
here, so sudden. Mist, wreathing from the earth. Now the
night.

The dark is peopling with illseen forms . . .

CAMBYSES. Say where you have been. Tell Lord Cambyses.

ATHDARK. Why ask, if thou see all?

CAMBYSES. Oh, sharp. Cheek of the lad. Why tell? Sin be for us
to know of, and for you to confess. Else how are your fathers,
and you, and I, at one? Bad son. Bad son. Tell Cambyses.
Tell your Lord.

ATHDARK. I have walked in a garden of Sin. I fell asleep. I
walked among strange gods. I spoke with Jezebel, in tongues
of Babel. She led me to a high place. She showed me her City,
shining on a hill. Then I heard the voice of the God of my
fathers. My eyes were opened. I saw I was on witches' mire.
In Cumri land. I came away. I came away!

CAMBYSES. So. Athdark fell asleep. He woke among strange
gods. Then from that waking, he woke back again: to the voice
of his own God?

ATHDARK. Yes! yes! Lord, pity me.

CAMBYSES. Good. Good. Well then. Now, from this waking too,
a deeper Athdark has to waken. All that while you slept and
waked and walked and waked again, a deeper deeper Athdark
lay in you asleep. Curled in you, deep, like a sleeping dog:
ears twitching at some sound that does not wake him, but he
hears; nostrils twitching at some scent that does not wake him,
but he'll know again. This deeper brother wake. I call on
him. Phwwwwwy . . . Phwwwwy . . . Tik tik tik . . .

*. . . From gathering forms, a like mimicry, as they tune into
the sounds of the night . . .*

WEREWOLVES. Phwwy phwwy . . . Tik tik tik . . . Hwy hwy
hwy hwy . . . PhwwwwwWWWww . . . Tik tik tik tik . . . Hwy
hwy hwy . . . Master . . . Cambyses . . . Hunter of the Night . . .

ONE (*the voice is* WIDOW FLAX). Deep through our sleep thy
cry came down to us . . .

ANOTHER (*voice is* LITORIUS *in his older, rustic mode as
wolf*). We awake with gladness . . .

A THIRD (*unmistakably the Pastor* AGRICOLA, *and deathly
soft*). Alleluia . . .

CAMBYSES. Brother and sisterhood, I love you all . . .
Manclothes away . . . So . . . So . . . So . . . So . . .

ATHDARK. Not want . . . Not want to . . .

CAMBYSES. Mark each our own with our own water . . .
So . . . So . . .

ATHDARK. Leave me sleeping . . .

CAMBYSES. Lady Mother. Good round Moon. Full, ripe, touch
all our hide to life. Man shrink inward. Wolf stand outward.
Skin in, out pelt! Hairs itch and bristle! Wolf, wake!

ATHDARK. No! No! No . . .

CAMBYSES. City on a hill you say? Had this a name? In their
tongue of Babel? Dinas Maros? Great Citadel? We've never
feasted there. We've never found our way so deep in Cumri
land as their forbidden city. Dinas Maros . . . Dinas Maros . . .
forbidden city.

Dinas Maros . . . Dinas Maros . . .

ATHDARK. Leave me . . . Leave me . . .

CAMBYSES. Phwwy, phwwy . . . Hwy hwy hwy hwy, tik tik
tik . . . Brother Snout, you left a spoor could guide us
there . . .

ATHDARK. Oh let me sleep . . .

   . . . *The illseen forms begin to prowl and seethe* . . .

*[LITORIUS. Master? I remember . . . Once I fell on a woman
gathering peas. Twilight it were. Across a low stone hedge
I'd watched her. Then . . . I sprang!

CAMBYSES. Serve her right. For gathering peas by such bad
light . . . Remember . . .

AGRICOLA. I leapt on a child . . . When would that be? By a
stone bridge. Little girl. With flowers from a meadow. I left
her, corpse among her flowers . . .

CAMBYSES. Remember . . .

WIDOW FLAX. We are wolf. We are free. No act we cannot do.
Soundless, and cannot be told from the dark.] Swift as the
wind, one bound on this earth, all distance leaps to me.

* In the Almeida production the passage between square brackets was
cut.   DR.

LITORIUS. Master! I go wolf journey! Scent, scent, smell British blood! Dinas Maros, Dinas Maros . . .

AGRICOLA. Alleluia!

WIDOW FLAX. Master, such joy!

CAMBYSES. Daughter? Joy? Ay. But Duty. God's Work is joy. The joy is in His Duty that we do. Brother?!

WOLVES. Ehmen. Ehmen. (*But* ATHDARK *silent* . . .)

CAMBYSES. We are the shapes of His Wrath. And Wrath must work. Those in that city are not of God's Pattern. Rake at their hides with our claws God gave us! Harrow with our fangs, till the bowels of their filth gush from them tumbled and uncoiling; till the lungs of them, livers, lights and wombs of all their darkness spill like offal in their own gutters; till their limbs lie, parted, quivering, unknowable for pieces of Man. I tell you. Flood may come, sweep all this sinful world away; for us alone His Ark stands ready. If we are worthy! We must merit! Work, then! When did I ever tell you wrong? When did Cambyses ever lead his hosts astray? To Dinas Maros! Work His Will!

LITORIUS. Master? How do I tell my maw as wolf be larger than my mouth as man by day? My mouth do always feel the same . . .

CAMBYSES. Quick! After! Our brother shows the way!

ACT FOUR

Scene One

Night. The high place. ATHDARK *half-wolf. British music from afar.*

ATHDARK. Here she was . . . And here she was . . . Her track and mine this morning . . . This is the high place . . . Oh Lady I did wrong to leave you, Lady help me find you now . . . My skin . . . My skin! No! No . . . ! I smell the blood of a British man . . . Old . . . Freshly dead . . . Beneath this ground . . . Leave him. Lady . . . ? Help me . . . What music's that? Lady . . . ? Lady . . . ? She's walked this way . . . Here . . . And here . . . And back again . . . Oh Lady Lady lead me to you! Help me stay a man! Down, wolf, down, down! Music . . . Dance and singing yonder . . . Lady, are you there? I want to dance and sing! They'll not let Athdark in. A Saxon man . . . They know who they are. Who am I?! . . . Here she trod . . . And here she trod . . . Follow, follow . . . Who's that? Our Nine of Wolves, come loping after . . . No! No! Oh hurry, hurry, save my love . . .

Scene Two

Music, dancing off. CEIRIAD *comes alone, in white.*

CEIRIAD. Lady. Lady of Mercy. Lady of Healing. Lady of Grief. It did not come to me calling itself Love, this burning. If Love be its name, Love I have. And in the heart. It makes no sense. And I'm more foolish than the foolishest girl ever brought little clay heart to Your shrine. But I'm glad. Folly or no, I thank You for it, Lady of All Grace. Whatever pain's to come, You have heard my prayer. I have once known the glorious burning in the heart.

ATHDARK (*somewhere unseen*). Lady . . . Lady . . .

CEIRIAD. He is here! My stranger! He is here he is here!

ATHDARK. Help me . . .

CEIRIAD. My love? Why do you hide from me? Sir?

ATHDARK (*ill-seen in shadows*). Not Deenio. Not Deenio. Tell me my name . . . Help me!

CEIRIAD. What are you saying? Oh my love — Do not flinch from me!

ATHDARK. Save me! My name! Help poor Deenio! Tell Deenio my name of a man!

CEIRIAD. You hide like a wounded beast. You are hurt. I know it. And the hurt makes you ugly. My love my love it does not matter! Where are you? No name by which to call you . . . But Man. Brother. Friend. Stand out into the light. I love you!

ATHDARK (*emerging*). I have left my name with my coat on the ground. I have no name when I come this journey, but snout, tooth, fang, claw . . . Tell me the name of the man I am! Or I do what I do. I come now. Here I am. Lady, pity me . . .

He sinks his teeth into her throat. Both fall. Music turns to a scream. SULGWEN *comes.*

SULGWEN. Ceiriad! A Heiriad!

ATHDARK. The Nine of Wolves . . . !

SULGWEN. Lady . . . ?

ATHDARK. I found her.

SULGWEN. You . . .

ATHDARK. What beast have tore this lovely lady?

SULGWEN. What beast indeed?

ATHDARK. Not me!

SULGWEN. Ay! Run! All of you! Ravage, and run!

A Heiriad a Heiriad . . . For this you healed him? To bring his havoc to our city? and savage your grace? Let Sulgwen lay you straight . . . And cover your white body . . .

Ay ay . . . Once there was a princess . . . Doomed at birth by a cruel curse . . . To lie asleep for ever, on the bed of a high

mountain lake . . . Heiriad a Heiriad . . . Oh a man would
come. A prince, and wake her. In a story there's always that.
And in a story there's always one condition. That prince,
she must never let him touch her with iron. The years passed.
Sure enough one day, a prince came wandering, stranger to
that green land. Handsome, golden of hair. All that. And in
the manner of princes in stories, on the shore of that high
mountain lake sat he, singing a song to his alien harp. At the
sound of his strange singing the lady awoke. She rose through
the waters. Black streaming hair, white skin, lips red as blood,
up she rose from the lake before him. She'd have scared me
half to death. But he was a man. Sap headier than sense. And
she was a woman, just awake. She saw he was tall and fair
like an angel. Each was that enthralled with the other, there
was no telling them; and in time they were married. The
kingdoms were joined, her green land, and the kingdom of
the golden-headed man. With great rejoicing, and hope, the
kingdoms were joined. Soon, one, then another, their children
began to be born. Strange daughters and sons, cantankerous
and squalling. Oh, and she taught him healing with herbs.
All that green wisdom we hear so much about. Till one day,
one day, he and her had words. And he hit her, with the
horsebit he had in his hand. I suppose they were tacking up to
go riding, as king and queen do in a story. Anyway, there he
had hit her, and the horsebit was iron. And with iron she must
never be touched. In that instant, all that their marrying had
brought them vanished. She, to thin air. A shriek on the wind,
she was gone. Their children fell asunder, to dust before his
very eyes. Scattered on the wind, and gone. All their palace
crumbled, to mounds in the grass. Sleep, lady, sleep . . .

Their two kingdoms are at war to this day. He, like a stone
man now, stands ever calling on that high lake shore: My love,
my love, my lady my love my love, oh come to me again,
my love my love. I'll not hit you this time. Well, not with
iron. She lies bleeding, eyes open, on the bed of that high
lake for ever.

Ceiriad a Heiriad . . . Ma vróghona, ma vróghona . . .

Scene Three

Funeral drum. Celts, grim in black, bearing each a body or emblem of their dead, call out the names.

ONE. Mắr'uos: Tegh'yírnacos, máppo Donachắti.

ALL. Di'uóvis ádrod'hếtor.

A SECOND. Mắr'uos: Aláunos, máppo Morghét'yudoi.

ALL. Di'uóvis ádrod-hếtor.

A MOTHER. Mắr'ui. Uíndos. Brắnos. Uí'o'yes Uõ'rón'ui'oi.

She mourns two small children . . .

ALL. Di'uóvis ádrod'héntor.

LUGOVELIN. Mắr'ua. Mắr'ua. Ceiriad. S'uếror. Ceiriad. Mốrighnā. Ceiriad. U'rắkō. Ceiriad a Heiriad, inigh'yéna Llir'yos, righántī Vretáni'yās!

CELTS. Heiriad! Heiriad! Righántī Vretáni'yās! Di'uõvis ádrod'hétor!

LUGOVELIN. Sássonikhi! Klu'ét'hwes! Pwid mắnet an dligétos ar ũlati'yo pwan dál'ya'ssáte? Sássonikhi! Pwi ahóctu mai swéro genéthli'yo?! Sássonikhi! Pwo ahóctu swér'ya sérachta?! In pwiắ tīrā?! Ad'heb ró'hwes!

SULGWEN. Saxons! What is your title to the land you have taken? Who are your people now? Now to what land is your desire? Answer!!

LUGOVELIN. Nẽts ád'heb ró'hwes, vélsint nẽs ád'heb ród'mos . . .

SULGWEN. Until you answer, here is our answer:

Raise each a clawlike hand in bloodstained salute above the dead —

Scene Four

ATHDARK *enters. (Unshared reality. Celts bear their dead away.)*

ATHDARK. Not me. Not me done that. Coat I were wearing.

That coat. Led me astray. I've took it off. I rolled it off. In the dew. Wolfskin, I said, thou tell me wrong. Thou lie on the ground. There's better. Lie. Lie still. There's better. And Stars, I said, you stand away. Stars you stand back! Stop your laughing! Quiet all you stars! Stars be still. There's better. Stars you stay there, small, and far . . . I must see about burying this mother . . .

He cries out. Someone is here.

LITORIUS. It's only me. Squire Litorius.

ATHDARK. Oh . . . Squire . . .

LITORIUS. The Pastor here? I'd thought he might be.

ATHDARK. Pastor . . . ?

LITORIUS. Spot of bother with your farm I see. I'd lend a hand. But I must hurry. Need the Pastor's help deciphering this. Some sort of letter from the Emperor. 'To the Communities of Britain' . . . (*Gone.*)

ATHDARK. Letter? From my Emperor? Squire? Squire Litorius? Wait . . . !

Scene Five

Community: the Pastor AGRICOLA; AGNES *his wife, pregnant; the bent* OLD FARMER *comes;* LITORIUS, *then* ATHDARK *hurrying after.*

AGRICOLA (*quietly*). This is a copy of a letter the Emperor has written to all the cities in our province. I will read what it says.

My beloved communities of Britain. You will have heard by now of the havoc and waste the Goth is wreaking upon our continent of Europe. He has reached the Alps. If he cross south, assure yourselves he will be overcome. We shall prevail. But to that end, and you will see the need, we must withdraw all military forces to the continental mainland. This need will not last long. Indeed, by the time this letter reaches you, I am sure that order and the Roman Peace will have been restored. When that is so, of course the military presence will

be returned to you, and to the support of your civil power.
Till then — I emphasize, only till then — you communities of
Britain must see to your own defence. I remain your loving
Emperor in Jesus the Christ, Honorius Flavius Augustus
Caesar, Ravenna, March, this Year of Grace, four hundred and
ten.

Silence.

AGNES. Where's that Rome? Which way is Rome?!

She cries Romeward:

You brought us here! You rooted us up from our own lands!
You herded us —

LITORIUS. Now now young lady —

AGNES. Don't you Lady me. What lady have ever I been to you?
My grandmother sat in chains! She were four year old!
Amongst her folk, mothers, fathers, children, all in chains!
Shipped like beasts from their own land, to be parted regardless
of kin, stationed on some Imperial plan along your borders!
For a uniform, a pett of stolen land —

AGRICOLA. Agnes woman, hush —

AGNES. I will not hush!

AGRICOLA. That was nothing to do with Squire Litorius
himself nor with anybody living now. All that was
generations past . . .

AGNES. So might it be. We're living now. Here, where that past
has put us —

LITORIUS. You must adapt. You must seize this future as a
challenge. And meet it with a new maturity —

AGNES. Well for you! Well for you, Imperial mighty Power!
Set us and 'native British at each others' throats: now,
forsake us naked to their rage. And have the gall to preach at
us! Covenant, you call this? Take everything away from a
folk? Land? Roots? All our belonging? Pluck us up and
plant us in this foreign island where we have no belonging?
Where we must rob and savage to thrive at all? Then give us

no defence? Covenant?! Not even a name. British, and not. Saxon, and not. Roman, and not. Who shall we say that we are now?

LITORIUS. It's you must see to that. If you'll pardon me, I must hurry and warn my wife.

He goes. Silence.

OLD FARMER. We must take stock of what weapons we have. We have a task to do. In name of Rome, a province to defend. We shall show them. They perfidious Romans. Eee, when their war wi 'Goths be done, and they're mopping all up, they shall glance to usward. 'Ah' they shall say, 'they Saxons. Whatever happened they Saxon folk we dumped in old Britannia?' 'Oh' some'll say, 'Saxons is it? Don't bother calling they to mind. 'Kelts have 'Slahtered all they Saxons in their beds. Good riddance.' Then they'll see. They'll see, with such surprise, such wonder and astonishment and shäme. 'Yond wall,' they'll say. 'Lewk at yond wall. Whoever have rebuilded that? So stout, so grand. Never they Saxons. We never thought . . .'

AGRICOLA. Ay grandad. Happen.

OLD FARMER. Everywhere it be broke, we shall restore it! Every milecastle shall be raised high again! Every tower —

AGNES. Grandad Griseholm, speak some sense!

OLD FARMER. Sense. When did A ever speak aught else? Ha? When did old man Griseholm ever tell you wrong, heh? When did —

ATHDARK. Look! Look. A light from the tower!

AGNES. Roman messages. No business of us now.

ATHDARK. Pug. Na . . . A battle . . . No, wait . . . Mag. Na . . . A big battle . . . I understand it! It's Latin, clear to me as my own tongue! It's Latin, and I understand it!

OLD FARMER. Well what does it say lad?

ATHDARK. Look! Vic. Ti . . . Defeated! A big battle. The defeated —

AGNES. Defeated who? The Goths?

ATHDARK. He's telling us! Su. Pugna magna victi su. Yes! In a big battle have been defeated . . .

AGNES. Who?!

ATHDARK. Wait for the end of the word! SuMUS, we; suUNT, they. Pugnah magnah victi su . . . Why has he stopped?

OLD FARMER. Right bloody language for information.

ATHDARK. Mus! Mus, look! I understand! SuMUS, we! Victi suMUS, we are defeated!

I understand it! A whole Latin sentence, and I understand it! We —

Silence.

OLD FARMER. Well brother Athdark. If ay that turn of speech had meaning, meaning has it now. You bring the bad word. Battle where, no matter. Who versus whom, no matter. We be the losers.

AGNES. What's that he's saying now?

AGRICOLA. Urbs . . . Roma . . . The city of Rome . . .

They watch . . .

. . . is no more.

Silence.

ATHDARK. On 'tower, look. The light's gone out.

OLD FARMER. Ay. And on 'next. Tower to tower. Along the Wall, look. Towers that still stand. The lights go out. Here come some night.

Silence.

AGNES. What do we do now?

AGRICOLA. I don't know.

OLD FARMER. I know what they Cumri 'll do. This land'll be acrawl wi they by morning. Not take they long to scent a carcase. Squire's Big House look. In flames already. I must see my lambs be safe. Pastor you do the same.

ATHDARK (*alone*). I must bury —

Goes.

Scene Six

Flames, smoke. LITORIUS *staggering with armfuls of \valuables;*
PRISCILLINA *drags a strongbox.*

LITORIUS. Priscillina? What have you in that box?

PRISCILLINA. Money, what do you think? We have to have
money! We're going to need so much money!

LITORIUS. Money? Have your years in Britannia taught you
nothing? Currency is an illusion; the bottom will fall out of
that! Gold, woman! Silver! What grows in value! The Parable
of the Talents, woman! Investment! Hurry, hurry! As much
gold and silverware as you can rescue! Quick! While there's
road still open to the sea!

PRISCILLINA. I daren't go back in there! The Selts will rape me!

LITORIUS. Only from the west! I mean in the North Wing you'll
be safe. But you must hurry! The peasants can hold out only
so long! Anything that we can sell to wealthy people! Trade
where the wealth is, that's the secret! Move!

PRISCILLINA. I hate rebellions.

LITORIUS. Pity we can't bring the mosaics. — Saxons? How you
doing there? Let's have some brawn in it! That's the spirit!
Good doughty Saxons! Don't give those swivel-eyed Brits one
inch! Not an inch, do you heah? Fight, Saxons, fight! For
your fathers! For your heritage! — Priscillina, shift yourself!

  PRISCILLINA *comes clattering with candlesticks, goblets etc.*

LITORIUS. Quick. To the sea . . .

PRISCILLINA. The servants!

LITORIUS. Leave them. We've not the room!

PRISCILLINA. Ohh!! Everywhere you've taken me our house has
been burned down! Everywhere we go there's trouble!
Hungary. Egypt. Spain . . . Why is the world so full of wicked
people?! Why is there so much violence?!

Scene Seven

Night still. ATHDARK *alone; his sword.*

ATHDARK. Rome . . . ? Gone . . . ? Spathum, sword . . . No duty
for you now. Rome. Gone. All that. Nothing.

. . . Her Wall is dark. Now Flood shall come. Who were it said?
Flood for the sinful world, for us His Ark . . . No Ark. The
Flood, for me.

. . . Old Hadrian. Mass of his masonwork. Black there, in 'light
of the stars. Little he knows: castle by castle, limestone,
turves, timber, Tyne to Solway, his crumbling have begun.

. . . Land. Dark. Phwwy phwwy. Tik tik tik. Land so still. . . .
Beck. Flows on. She saw Rome come. Little she know, she
have borne Rome away. Ahvona; current, stream . . . All this
land now. Foe to me. How shall I be neighbour, who have
been such fiend to these? There were such damage. There were
such bloody slaughter done. And I killed the lovely lady. She
was healing me . . . I do as the Good Word bids me. Spathum,
sword, I make a blade of you. To shear the clay.

. . . Stars. So far. So cold. . . . Spathum, sword: shall be a
spade. PhwwwwWWWwww . . . Tik . . . Tik . . . No. Wolf. No.
. . . They Welsh'll come . . . Wolf. No. Rest there on the
ground. Dream, that. I must wake now. I must wake. Stand.
Dig my garden. Spade. Spade. Who's there . . . ? Soon be
day . . .

He is standing now, the beginnings of a man.

A Note on Pronunciation and Sound

Narratively, three languages are spoken in the play: the Latin of
the NCO, an ur-Germanic of the 'Saxon' community, and the
old Celtic language of the British natives. These are represented
by different sorts of English. (What language(s) Litorius speaks,
and in what social dialect(s), is a fascinating question that I leave
open. The Litorii of this world really speak only English, plus a
smattering of native lingo.)

'Saxon' is strictly a misnomer, but it's the term that the Roman
administration used for Northern Germanic peoples in general.
The 'Saxon' English of this play is dense and packed, and
confined mainly to vocabulary of Germanic origin, with a few
significant Latin borrowings. The pastor Agricola will have
learned Latin at a European university. All these people, in
werewolf mode, regress to an archaic, rustic idiom, as their texts
suggest.

The Celtic English of this play is more sinuous and melodic. The
sentence-structures occasionally reflect the syntax of the Celtic
languages themselves. A character's name is sometimes heard with
its first consonant softened: *a Hulgwen* for 'Oh, Sulgwen'. This
happens in Irish and Welsh to this day.

Actors will ask, in which 'accents' are these various modes of
English spoken? My first answer is that characters are people,
and people don't have 'accents', they have *speech*. My next
answer is, that existing 'tunes' of spoken English — Welsh,
'Northern', and so on — set up the wrong contemporary
resonances. My third answer is that the 'tune' should be drawn
from the text, not imposed upon it. For all that, the question
will be asked, and some sort of guidance has to be given. So my
final answer is, that for the 'Saxon' language I have fused certain
Northern English 'tunes' with Northern Irish idiom, and vice
versa; and for the Celtic language I have, more delicately, blended
Welsh and Southern Irish tune and idiom in a similar way. It is
up to the actor to hear the text exactly, and speak as the text

suggests. This, of itself, will create the music I need.

The few snatches of Latin that are heard in the play should be given in schoolboy pronunciation: *c* and *g* hard, *s* light, the long *u* of *u*sum and Spirit*us* like English *oo*. A schoolteacher of Latin (dying breed) would be the best adviser on this.

The few isolated words of Cumri language that Athdark learns are respectable reconstructions — the most likely 5th-century forms that would have yielded for instance *afon* and *mynydd* today. In *nemeta* the *e* is short, the *a* is long; in *deruoi* the *e* is short, the *u* is like the long Latin *u* above; in *avona* the first *a* is long and carries the stress. The *ma vróghona* at the end of Sulgwen's long story is tentative Cumric for 'my grief'; the first *o* is long, and carries the stress. After the werewolves have finally alienated the Celts, and the separation between the two cultures is made unbridgeable, I give the Celts an entire scene in their own language. This is a reconstruction of my own, going much further than a real philologist would dare, and drawing on the oldest forms we have of certain personal names, and — for Lugovelin's *Sassonikhi* speech — three lines from a much later Welsh poem, *The Great Prophecy of Britain*. I have marked in the text how I feel this should all be pronounced. The apostrophe in the middle of certain words is there merely to separate sounds that otherwise might be run together. The speeches mean:

— Dead: Tierney, son of Donoghue.

— May he be returned to the gods.

— Dead: Alun, son of Meredith.

— May he be returned to the gods.

— Dead: Finn, Bran, sons of Goronwy.

— May they be returned to the gods.

— Dead. Dead.
  Ceiriad. Sister.
  Ceiriad. Virgin.
  Ceiriad. Wife.
  Ceiriad, oh Ceiriad,
  daughter of Lear,
  queen of Britain.

— Oh Ceiriad! Oh Ceiriad!
  Queen of Britain.
  May she be returned to the gods.

— Saxons!
  Listen!
  What is your title
  to-the land that you-have-taken?
  Saxons!
  Who now are your kin?
  Saxons!
  Where now (is) your desire-to-be?
  In which land?
  Answer give!

  Until answer you-give,
  thus we answer (we-) give.

What is important in the playing of this scene is that the *emotions*
should be clear. The language should sound grim, and alien, and
frightening; and there should be not one sound in it that
resembles that in any modern foreign language that we might
know.

Last, there is an occasional oddity in the punctuation of the
'Saxon' English. Two dots over an *a* mean what they would in
German spelling. An apostrophe at the *beginning* of a word
suggests that strange sound in modern Northern English where a
the has been suppressed yet its absence is made somehow audible.

An Acting Note

On the question of the werewolves, it can never be right to use
wolfmasks or werewolf costume. These human characters
experience themselves as wolves. In a term much used during
Almeida rehearsals, the transformation to werewolf is an 'acting
problem'.

DR

WATERSTONE'S BOOKSELLERS LTD

339426